# Alles über die
# OLYMPISCHEN SPIELE

## All About the
## OLYMPICS

Von Nick Hunter

**OLMS**

**Abgebildete SportlerInnen** (von links nach rechts)
**Athletes as shown** (left to right)
S./p. 5: Dawn Harper, USA; Delloreen Ennis-London, Jamaika; LoLo
Jones, USA • S./p. 9: Mark Foster, Großbritannien/UK • S./p.12: Jared
Tallent, Australien/Australia; Alex Schwazer, Italien/Italy; Denis Nizhe-
gorodov, Russland/Russia • S./p.15: Victoria Pendleton, Großbritan-
nien/UK; Anna Meares, Australien/Australia • S./p.16: Tom Daley •
S./p.17: Steve Hooker, Australien/Australia • S./p.18: Matthias Steiner,
Deutschland/Germany • S./p.19: Ayumi Tanimoto, Japan; Lucie Decosse,
Frankreich/France • S./p.20: Nastia Liukin, USA/UK • S./p.21: Das ka-
nadische Ruderteam, vor Großbritannien (Bootsnummer 4, vorne im
Bild) und den USA (Bootsnummer 2, hinten im Bild)./Canada's rowing
team, in front of UK (boat no 4, foreground) and USA (boat no 2, back-
ground). • S./p.24: Joey Johnson, Kanada (Mitte, Trikotnummer 8)/
Canada (mid position, shirt number 8) • S./p.26: Lindsey Vonn, USA •
S./p.27: Kanadisches Eishockeyteam gegen die USA (Tor)./Canada's ice
hockey team against USA (in goal).

## Bibliografische Informationen
## der Deutschen Nationalbibliothek

Die Deutsche Nationalbibliothek verzeichnet diese Publikation
in der Deutschen Nationalbibliografie; detaillierte bibliografische
Daten sind im Internet über http://dnb.d-nb.de abrufbar.

BiLi – Zweisprachige Sachgeschichten für Kinder
in der Kollektion OLMS junior

Copyright für diese Ausgabe
© Georg Olms Verlag AG, Hildesheim 2011
Alle Rechte vorbehalten
Originalausgabe: *All About the Olympics* by Nick Hunter
Under Licence from Capstone Global Library Limited
Übersetzung aus dem Englischen: Cordula Seiter
Lektorat: Faith Clare Voigt

ISBN 978-3-487-08856-3

**www.olms-junior.de**

## Acknowledgements
We would like to thank the following for permission to reproduce
photographs: Corbis pp. 4 (epa/ Alessandro Della Bella), 5 (epa/
Kay Nietfeld), 7 (Bettmann), 9 (epa/ John Mabanglo), 10 (epa/ Kay
Nietfeld), 11 (Stefan Matzke), 13 (epa/ Gero Breloer), 14 (epa/ Kay
Nietfeld), 19 (epa/ Simela Pantzartzi), 20 (Andrew Mills), 25 (epa/
Oliver Weiken), 26 (Reuters/ Stefano Rellandini); Getty Images pp. 8, 17
(Mark Dadswell), 18 (Al Bello), 23 (AFP/ Michael Kappeller), 28 (Julian
Finney); Press Association Images pp. 6 (AP Photo/Thanassis Stavrakis),
12 (AP Photo/ Luca Bruno), 21 (LANDOV), 27 (ABACA); Rex Features
p. 15, 16, 24 (Sipa Press), 22 (Rex Features/ Warren King); 29 (Rex
Features).

Cover photograph of the Beijing 2008 Torch Relay reproduced with
permission of Corbis (Xinhua Press/ Qi Heng).

Every effort has been made to contact copyright holders of material
reproduced in this book. Any omissions will be rectified in subsequent
printings if notice is given to the publisher.

## Disclaimer

All the Internet addresses (URLs) given in this book were valid at the
time of going to press. However, due to the dynamic nature of the
internet, some addresses may have changed, or sites may have changed
or ceased to exist since publication. While the author and publisher
regret any inconvenience this may cause readers, no responsibility for
any such changes can be accepted by either the author or the publisher.

Edited by Dan Nunn and Catherine Veitch
Designed by Richard Parker
Picture research by Hannah Taylor
Originated by Capstone Global Library
Printed in China by South China Printing Company Ltd

# Inhalt
## Contents

Einige Wörter sind fett gedruckt, **so wie hier.** Wenn du in den Worterklärungen nachsiehst, findest du heraus, was sie bedeuten.

Some words are shown in bold, **like this**. You can find out what they mean by looking in the glossary.

# Willkommen bei den Olympischen Spielen
## Welcome to the Olympics

Die Olympischen Spiele sind ein Sport**fest**. Menschen aus der ganzen Welt treffen sich, um teilzunehmen und den Sportereignissen zuzuschauen. Die Spiele finden alle vier Jahre statt. Sie beginnen mit einer **Eröffnungszeremonie**.

The Olympic Games are a **festival** of sport. People from around the world meet to play and watch sport. The Olympics take place every four years. They begin with the **opening ceremony**.

Die Eröffnungszeremonie ist eine farbenfrohe Feier, die die Olympischen Spiele einleitet.

The opening ceremony is a colourful party that starts the Olympics.

Diese Athletinnen laufen so schnell sie können, um den Wettkampf zu gewinnen.

These athletes are running as fast as they can to win this race.

Mehr als 10 000 Sportler nehmen an den Olympischen Spielen teil. Jeder **Athlet** versucht, in seiner Sportart der Beste zu sein. Das **Motto** der Olympischen Spiele lautet „Schneller, Höher, Stärker".

There are more than 10,000 **athletes** at the Olympics. The athletes try to be the best at their sport. The **motto** of the Olympic Games is "Faster, Higher, Stronger".

# Die ersten Olympischen Spiele
# The first Olympics

Die ersten Olympischen Spiele begannen vor mehr als 2 500 Jahren. **Athleten** aus verschiedenen Gegenden des **antiken Griechenland** trafen sich an einem Ort namens Olympia. Noch heute können wir das **Stadion** in Olympia besichtigen, in dem die ersten Spiele stattfanden.

The first Olympic Games began more than 2,500 years ago. **Athletes** from different parts of **ancient Greece** met at a place called Olympia. We can still see the **stadium** at Olympia where the first Olympics took place.

Dies ist der Eingang zum ersten
Olympia-Stadion in Griechenland.
This is the entrance to the first
Olympic stadium in Greece.

6

Wir können uns auch Statuen von antiken, griechischen Athleten anschauen. Diese antike, griechische Statue zeigt einen Mann, der einen **Diskus** wirft. Diskuswerfen gehört auch heute noch zu den Olympischen Sportarten.

We can also see statues of ancient Greek athletes. This ancient Greek statue shows a man throwing a **discus**. Discus throwing is still a part of the Olympics now.

Statuen helfen uns herauszufinden, wie die Olympischen Spiele im alten Griechenland abliefen.

Statues help us to find out about what happened at the ancient Greek Olympics.

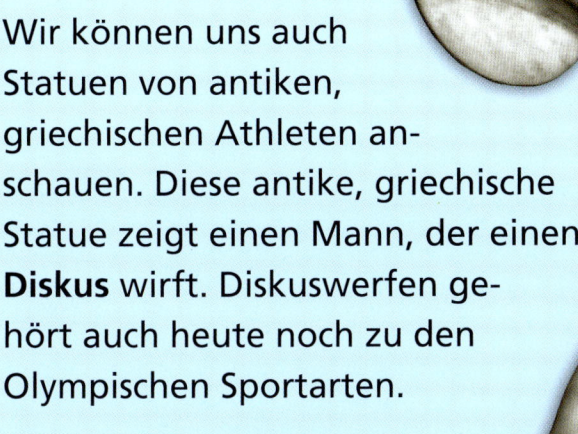

# Die modernen Olympischen Spiele
## The modern Olympics

Die ersten modernen Olympischen Spiele wurden 1896 veranstaltet. An den ersten modernen Spielen nahmen keine Sportlerinnen teil. Heutzutage sind fast die Hälfte aller **Athleten** Frauen.

The first modern Olympic Games were held in 1896. There were no women **athletes** at the first modern Olympics. Now, nearly half of all the athletes are women.

In Athen in Griechenland trafen sich Sportler zu den ersten modernen Olympischen Spielen.

Athletes met in Athens, Greece for the first modern Olympic Games.

Bei der **Eröffnungs-zeremonie** ziehen Athleten aus jedem Land zusammen ein.

Athletes from each country march together at the **opening ceremony**.

Die Olympischen Spiele werden jedes Mal in einem anderen Land auf der Welt veranstaltet. 2008 fanden die Spiele in Peking, also in China, statt. Die Athleten kamen aus 204 Ländern der ganzen Welt.

The Olympics are held in different cities around the world. In 2008, the Games were in Beijing, China. Athletes came from 204 countries around the world.

# Die Symbole der Olympischen Spiele
## Symbols of the Olympics

Das Olympische Feuer ist ein **Symbol** der Olympischen Spiele. Es wird zu Beginn der Spiele entzündet. Das Olympische Feuer brennt so lange bis die Olympischen Spiele zu Ende sind.

The Olympic Flame is a **symbol** of the Olympic Games. The flame is lit at the start of the Games. It stays lit until the Olympics have finished.

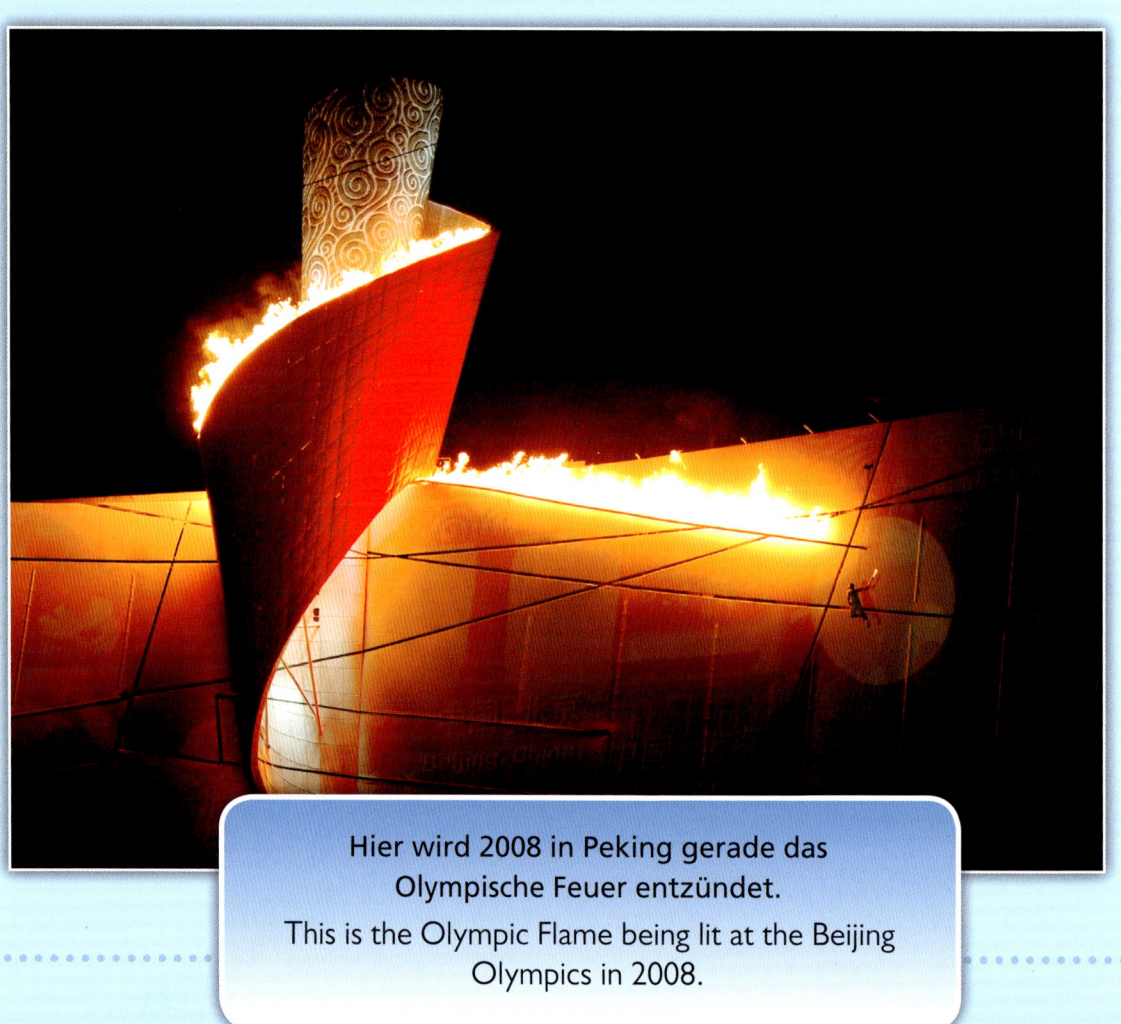

Hier wird 2008 in Peking gerade das Olympische Feuer entzündet.

This is the Olympic Flame being lit at the Beijing Olympics in 2008.

Auf der Olympia-**Flagge** sieht man fünf Ringe. Die Flagge ist ein Symbol für alle Länder der Erde. Zu den Olympischen Spielen kommen alle Länder zusammen.

The Olympic **Flag** has five rings on it. The flag is a symbol of all the countries in the world. All countries come together for the Olympic Games.

# Teilnahme
## Taking part

Die Besten ihrer Sportart bekommen **Medaillen**. Die Gewinner erhalten eine Goldmedaille. Sie werden Olympische **Champions** genannt. Die Nächstbesten gewinnen Silber- und Bronzemedaillen.

People who do best in their sport are given **medals**. The winners get gold medals. They are called Olympic **champions**. The people who come next win silver and bronze medals.

Goldmedaille
gold medal

Die chinesische Sportlerin Zhang Yining legt bei den Olympischen Spielen 2008 in Peking den Olympischen Eid ab.

Chinese athlete Zhang Yining takes the Olympic Oath at the Beijing 2008 Olympics.

Zu Beginn jeder Spiele legt ein Sportler den Olympischen **Eid** ab. Er oder sie verspricht, sich an die Regeln zu halten und fair zu kämpfen. Fairness ist bei den Olympischen Spielen sehr wichtig.

One **athlete** takes the Olympic **Oath** at the start of every Olympic Games. He or she promises to follow the rules and play fairly. Fair play is very important to the Olympics.

# Schneller
## Faster

Sprinter gewinnen, indem sie schneller laufen als die anderen **Athleten** in ihrem Rennen. Der Sieger des Olympischen 100-Meter-Laufs wird der ‚schnellste Mann der Welt' oder die ‚schnellste Frau der Welt' genannt.

Runners win by running faster than the other **athletes** in their race. The winner of the Olympic 100-metres race is called the fastest man or woman in the world.

Usain Bolt aus Jamaika gewann den 100-Meter-Lauf bei den Spielen in Peking.

Usain Bolt of Jamaica won the 100-metres race at the Beijing Olympics.

Radrennfahrer beugen sich tief über ihren Lenker, um so schnell wie möglich zu sein.

Cyclists crouch low over their bikes to go as fast as possible.

Radrennfahrer müssen kräftig in die Pedale treten und ihr Rad sorgfältig lenken, um eine Gold**medaille** zu gewinnen. Bahn-radfahrer müssen aufpassen, dass sie die schräge Bahn nicht hinabrutschen.

Cyclists have to pedal fast and steer their bikes carefully to win a gold **medal**. They have to be careful not to slide down the sloping track.

# Höher
## Higher

Turmspringer springen von einem hohen Sprungbrett hinab ins Becken. Sie versuchen im Wasser zu landen, ohne dass es zu sehr spritzt. Wertungsrichter entscheiden, wer der beste Springer ist.

Divers jump into the pool from a high board. They try not to make a big splash when they land in the water. Judges decide who is the best diver.

Turmspringer drehen sich und springen kopfüber ins Becken.
Divers twist and turn over as they dive.

Stabhochspringer können höher springen als ein Doppeldeckerbus hoch ist.

Pole vaulters can jump higher than a double-decker bus.

Einige **Athleten** versuchen möglichst hoch zu springen. Ein **Stabhochspringer** nimmt einen Stab zu Hilfe, um über eine hohe Latte zu springen. Die Latte darf nicht herunterfallen.

Some **athletes** see how high they can jump. A **pole vaulter** uses a pole to help him jump over a high bar. He must not make the bar fall down.

# Stärker

## Stronger

»»»»

Manche Sportler müssen sehr stark sein, um eine **Medaille** zu gewinnen. Gewichtheber stemmen Stangen mit schweren Metallscheiben an beiden Enden. Die Goldmedaille gewinnt, wer das schwerste Gewicht heben kann.

Some **athletes** need to be the strongest to win a **medal**. Weight-lifters lift bars with heavy blocks of metal on the ends. The one who can lift the most wins the gold medal.

Gewichtheber heben Gewichte, die schwerer sind als sie selbst.
Weightlifters lift weights that are heavier than they are.

Im Judo versucht ein Kämpfer den anderen zu Boden zu werfen. Die Kämpfer müssen geschickt und kräftig sein, um ihren **Gegner** zu besiegen.

In judo, one player tries to throw the other one on to the ground. The players need to be skilful and strong to beat their **opponents**.

# Trainieren für die Olympischen Spiele
## Training for the Olympics

Jeder **Athlet** bei den Olympischen Spielen muss sehr hart trainieren. **Turner** trainieren jeden Tag. Ihre Bewegungen müssen fließend und **graziös** sein, wenn sie eine **Medaille** gewinnen wollen.

Every **athlete** at the Olympic Games must train very hard. **Gymnasts** train every day. Their movements must be smooth and **graceful** for them to win **medals**.

Diese Turnerin hat jahrelang trainiert, um bei den Olympischen Spielen antreten zu können.
This gymnast has practised for many years to be at the Olympic Games.

Jeder Ruderer zieht ein Ruder, um das Boot durch das Wasser zu bewegen.

Each rower pulls one oar to help move the boat through the water.

Ruderer müssen kräftig und fit sein, um ihr Boot durch das Wasser zu rudern. Sie müssen als Team arbeiten, damit sie schneller vorankommen als die anderen Boote im Rennen.

Rowers have to be strong and fit to row their boat through the water. They must work as a team to go faster than the other boats in the race.

# Vorbereiten der Olympischen Spiele
## Staging the Olympics

Für die Olympischen Spiele werden viele verschiedene Gebäude errichtet. Für die Lauf-, Sprung- und Wurfsportarten wird ein **Stadion** gebaut. Das Stadion wird auch für die **Eröffnungszeremonie** der Spiele genutzt.

Lots of different buildings are built for the Olympic Games. A **stadium** is built for running, jumping, and throwing sports. The stadium is also used for the **opening ceremony** of the Olympics.

Olympia-Stadion
Olympic Stadium

Dies ist der Olympia-Park, der in London gebaut wird.
This is the Olympic Park being built in London.

Im Olympischen Dorf können Athleten aus verschiedenen Ländern Freunde finden.

Athletes can make friends from different countries in the Olympic Village.

Die **Athleten** kommen aus der ganzen Welt und brauchen während der Spiele alle einen Platz zum Wohnen. Darum wird für sie ein Olympisches Dorf gebaut.

**Athletes** from around the world all need somewhere to live during the Olympic Games. An Olympic Village is built for the athletes to live in.

# Die Paralympischen Spiele
## Paralympics

Die Olympischen Spiele sind für alle Menschen offen. Die Paralympischen Spiele finden gleich nach den Olympischen Spielen statt. Zu den Paralympischen Spielen kommen Sportler mit **Behinderung**. Einige dieser Sportler benutzen einen Rollstuhl.

The Olympics are for everyone. The Paralympics take place just after the Olympic Games. **Athletes** with **disabilities** come to the Paralympics. Some of these athletes use wheelchairs.

Diese Sportler spielen Rollstuhlbasketball.

These athletes are playing wheelchair basketball.

Viele der Sportarten bei den Paralympischen Spielen sind die gleichen wie bei den Olympischen Spielen. Eleanor Simmonds gewann 2008 zwei Gold**medaillen** im Schwimmen.

The Paralympics include many of the same sports as the Olympics. Eleanor Simmonds won two gold **medals** for swimming in 2008.

# Die Olympischen Winterspiele
## Winter Olympics

Auch die Olympischen Winterspiele finden alle vier Jahre statt. Die **Athleten** messen sich in all den Sportarten, für die sie Schnee und Eis brauchen. Skiläufer stehen auf langen Skiern, auf denen sie Berghänge hinuntergleiten.

The Winter Olympics also take place every four years. **Athletes** compete in sports that need snow and ice. Skiers stand on long skis to slide down the side of a mountain.

Abfahrt-Skiläufer können schneller werden als ein sehr schnell fahrendes Auto.

Downhill skiers can go faster than a speeding car.

Die kanadische
Eishockeymannschaft gewann
2010 die Goldmedaille.

Canada's team won the gold medal
for ice hockey in 2010.

Bei den Olympischen Winterspielen gibt es andere Sportarten als bei den Sommerspielen. Aber auch im Winter bekommen die Besten eine **Medaille**. 2010 fanden die Winterspiele in Vancouver in Kanada statt.

The sports at the Winter Olympics are different from the Summer Olympics. The winners still get **medals** for being the best. In 2010, the Winter Olympics took place in Vancouver, Canada.

# Willkommen in London
## Welcome to London

2012 kommen die Olympischen und Paralympischen Spiele nach London. London ist die Hauptstadt von Großbritannien. Die Olympia-**Maskottchen** werden die Sportler der Welt in London willkommen heißen.

The London 2012 Olympic Games and Paralympic Games will be held in London, the capital of the United Kingdom. The Olympic **mascots** will welcome the world's **athletes** to London.

Die Maskottchen der Londoner Spiele 2012 heißen Wenlock und Mandeville. Findest Du heraus, warum?

The mascots for the London 2012 Games are called Wenlock and Mandeville. Can you find out why?

Schau nach auf Seite 30.

Turn to page 30 for the answer.

Im Londoner Olympia-Stadion werden 80 000 Menschen den Olympischen Spielen 2012 zusehen können.

80,000 people will be able to watch the 2012 Games in the London Olympic Stadium.

Im neuen Olympia-**Stadion** in London werden viele Sportarten ausgetragen werden. Die Menschen im Stadion und auf der ganzen Welt werden den besten **Athleten** der Welt zujubeln.

Many sports will take place at the new Olympic **Stadium** in London. People in the stadium and across the world will cheer the world's best **athletes**.

# Extra-Wissen zu den Olympischen Spielen
## Olympic facts

▶ Michael Phelps aus den Vereinigten Staaten von Amerika hat mehr Olympische Gold**medaillen** gewonnen als irgendein anderer Sportler. Er hat im Schwimmen 14 Gold**medaillen** errungen.

Michael Phelps of the United States has won more Olympic gold **medals** than anyone else. He has won 14 gold medals for swimming.

▶ 2016 werden die Olympischen Spiele in Rio de Janeiro in Brasilien ausgetragen. Die Spiele finden dann zum ersten Mal in Südamerika statt.

The Olympic Games in 2016 will be held in Rio de Janeiro, Brazil. These will be the first Olympics in South America.

▶ Bei den antiken Olympischen Spielen gab es einen Wettkampf, bei dem die Läufer eine Rüstung tragen mussten.

In the ancient Olympic Games, there was a race for runners wearing armour.

**Antworten von Seite 28:**
Wenlock wurde nach dem Dorf Much Wenlock in Shropshire, England, benannt. Dort gab es schon vor den Olympischen Spielen der Neuzeit ein Sport**fest**.

Mandeville wurde nach Stoke Mandeville in Buckinghamshire, England, benannt. 1948 gab es dort den ersten Wettkampf für **Athleten** mit **Behinderung**.

**Answers from page 28:**
Wenlock is named after the village of Much Wenlock, in Shropshire. A **festival** of sport was held there before the modern Olympics began.

Mandeville is named after Stoke Mandeville, in Buckinghamshire. The first competition for **athletes** with **disabilities** began there in 1948.

# Worterklärungen
## Glossary

**Antikes Griechenland**: Ort, an dem Menschen vor mehr als 2000 Jahren lebten, in dem Land, das wir heute Griechenland nennen.
**ancient Greece**: Place where people lived more than 2,000 years ago, in the country we now call Greece.

**Athlet**: Jeder, der Wettkampfsport treibt.
**athlete**: anyone that takes part in a sport

**Behinderung**: Etwas, das jemanden davon abhält, bestimmte Dinge zu tun, wie zum Beispiel, wenn jemand nicht sehen oder nicht gehen kann.
**disability**: Something that stops someone doing things, such as not being able to see or walk.

**Champion**: Gewinner bei einem sportlichen Wettkampf
**champion**: someone who wins at a sport

**Diskus**: Flache Scheibe, die geworfen wird. Sportler versuchen sie möglichst weit zu werfen.
**discus**: Flat disc that is thrown. An athlete sees how far he can throw the discus.

**Eid**: ein Versprechen
**oath**: a promise

**Eröffnungszeremonie**: Feier, mit der die Olympischen Spiele eröffnet werden.
**opening ceremony**: party that starts the Olympic Games

**Fest**: Feier
**festival**: party or celebration

**Flagge**: Ein Stück Stoff, das an einer Stange weht. Jedes Land hat eine Flagge in seinen eigenen Farben.
**flag**: Piece of cloth that is flown from a pole. Each country has a flag with different colours.

**Gegner**: Person, die du beim Sport zu besiegen versuchst.
**opponent**: Person who you are trying to beat at sport.

**Graziös**: wenn sich jemand anmutig und geschickt bewegt
**graceful**: moving smoothly and skilfully

**Maskottchen**: Figur oder Gegenstand, der den Menschen Glück bringen soll.
**mascot**: Person or thing that people have to bring them luck.

**Medaille**: Ein Stück Metall, das jemand bekommt, der bei etwas gewonnen hat.
**medal**: Piece of metal given to someone for winning something.

**Motto**: Worte, die die Ziele einer Gruppe zusammenfassen. Das Olympische Motto ist „Schneller, höher, stärker".
**motto**: Words that sum up the aims of a group. The Olympic motto is "Faster, Higher, Stronger".

**Stabhochspringer**: Sportler, der einen Stab verwendet, um über eine hohe Latte zu springen.
**pole vaulter**: Sportsperson who uses a pole to help lift him or her over a high bar.

**Stadion**: Ort, an den viele Menschen gehen, um einem Sportereignis zuzuschauen.
**stadium**: Place where lots of people go to watch sport.

**Symbol**: Gegenstand oder Bild, der bzw. das für die Menschen eine besondere Bedeutung hat.
**symbol**: Something that stands for something else.

# Mehr über die Olympischen Spiele
## Find out more

### Bücher

*WAS IST WAS, Band 93: Die Olympischen Spiele*
Edwin Klein (Tessloff, 2010)

*Rund um den Sport (Wieso? Weshalb? Warum?):
Spiel, Sport, Olympia*
Klaus Toedt (Ravensburger, 2004)

*Was Kinder wissen wollen.
Warum laufen Läufer links herum?
Verblüffende Antworten über Sport und Olympia*
Ulrike Berger (Velber, 2008)

### Websites

**www.dosb.de** – Das ist die offizielle Seite
des Deutschen Olympischen Sportbundes.

Bitte einen Erwachsenen um Hilfe, um im
Internet mehr herauszufinden.
Sucht nach ‚London 2012' oder
‚Olympische Spiele'. Du kannst auch nach
dem Namen deines Lieblingsathleten oder
deiner Lieblingssportart suchen.

### Books

*Athletics*
Rebecca Hunter (Franklin Watts, 2009)
*British Olympians*
Debbie Foy (Wayland, 2009)
*The London Olympics 2012*
Nick Hunter (Raintree, 2012)
*The Story of the Olympics*
Minna Lacey (Usborne, 2008)

### Websites

**www.london2012.com** – This is the
official website of the London Olympics.

To find out more on the Internet,
ask an adult to help you search for
"London 2012" or "Olympic Games".
You can also search using the name
of your favourite athlete or sport.